The Veil

Kai Catahan

BookLeaf
Publishing

India | USA | UK

Presentation by *BookLeaf Publishing*

Web: www.bookleafpub.com

E-mail: info@bookleafpub.com

ISBN: 9789358314977

First edition 2023

I dedicate this book to every single pain I've experienced. From the chronic pain I feel daily to the tears I cry when another has hurt me.

Thank you.

PREFACE

Hey, welcome! This is my first poetry book, but I've been meaning to write a book for years. Fantasy novels, poetry books, random passionate essays. I mainly write through my songwriting. I love to write, you know, and writing has always been a way for me to express myself and make sense of the world.

I hope you enjoy peaking through The Veil as you read this collection! See you on the other side.

A Mortician

I execute brick walls he built years ago,
Cremate all the skyscrapers,
Towering me.
That man never let me breathe.
Unclothing trees of their leaves and
Lowering lilacs from their mantle pieces.

A piece of me is still embalming windows he
demanded I clean,
He drapes intestines over my gutted grave,
That man never let me leave.
He sealed my doors shut through burning wood,
My hoarse voice censored by my smile.

My boney digits decay as I claw his requiem
away from me,
Get away from me,
Get away from me,
Get away from me.

I will never mourn that man.

Who Hades Is

A god of the dead, though he is, he brings life
from the darkness. A traumatizing life do you
bare and yet how calm you seem, how?

I admire the way you stay peaceful with your
sarcastic laughter. The way your hugs are so
warm but people grant you the cold shoulder.
The "father" that I never had; that never left.
You said "I'll stay as long as needs be." But that
doesn't mean forever, strangely I don't mind
that.

 I don't mind your mystery, as harsh as it may
seem. Crinkled up paper from uninterpreted
dreams, you dance softly with the stars but stand
dormant near the core. The hand you guide me
with is like my own, expect I trust it. I trust it.

You once told me trust was wishful thinking and
I've been wishing ever since. Juvenile of me,
yes, but I still do. I suppose that's just something
I'll have to get used to. You say trust is beautiful
but so deceiving at times, isn't it glorious?

You often remind me that beauty is no match for me; for humans. Beauty is a hurdle that one must leap over social standards to pass. Such a teacher, you are. You deny it often. You once told me denial is a humans way of saying thank you, except it hurts.

You try to make me understand that you are more than a god of the dead, more than a father, more than a mystery and more than a teacher. Until I understand, I will continue to learn about your traumatizing life that you do bare; that I do bare and yet how calm I seem, how?

I'm The Librarian

A crashing wave of tears and bliss wash over me, every drop I become more vulnerable and every breath I feel more reachable. Although I may show great forbearance in many things it doesn't stop me from the vulnerability; I open up bookshops I once closed. I concluded no one would read any pages of the grand novels and complexities my mind conjures up.

I searched other bookshelves before opening my own library and found their tales more exciting. There was always beauty to a story's tragedy. The writing weeped for a second chance. A third chance. A fourth. A fifth.

And I'd read it over and over again. I'd expect a different ending.

The ending was always the same, however. The pages always extended to my neck. Shaking fingertips alike to arachnids crawling on my seams. They suffocated me. I'd try to shout out but a library doesn't allow that, I'd try to place a bookmark but it would always fall out. They'd never loosen the grip.

They'd never put down the pen.

Afterwards, I was always expected to rearrange the books, resort the pages, dust all the shelves and adorn them with gold, correct every word that was ever written down and bind them together. Because of this, I lost my love for books. I lost my love for books but I continued to be the librarian.

But now I've received the zephyrs of a new tale and my love for books is returning. This library allows me to shout. All the pages ask for my own and I hope I am vulnerable enough to allow every word to be read aloud.

Disloyal

She's constantly disciplined by handle bars,
Swinging back and forth,
She was built to plan lessons on scrunched up
wrappers disposed by her lineage. She will never
truly accept it.
Teaching dead brambles, what for?

This gruesome loss keeps her busy,
Forgetting to educate the warehouses she owns
as she manages the bungalows she rents,
I wish I could grade a three story building based
off the amount of stairs it makes me climb,
That would be disloyal.

She gave me homework on a train platform,
I was departing.
Disbelief will lead my rusty ladders to be
marked badly,
The same ladders I use to trip and swing,
Back and forth.
But, please, answer this for me:
Why continue to present to rowdy boys and
broken girls?
Why continue to guide street lights to an ozone
layer you acknowledge is present?

You correct road signs like they're suggestions,
She corrects me like I'm a suggestion,
But I love you.
I wish I could believe myself enough,
to not give you a second chance.
That would be disloyal.

Liminal

It was a subtle evening on November 32nd, an exile passed my lips as I drowned and I found myself in the space between the floorboards. You perceive insignificant colors there like yellow's only seen under rugs and between tiles. I go there often. Cages of anticipation that keep me within the present moment make my eyes gasp; I require release from that cage.

Fainting to step beyond the threshold, finally the waiting ceases. Waiting rooms surround my psyche; a soul constantly infected by being a patient for others to heal. I save myself intertwined with liminal escapes. Don't break this mask. The break rooms are my home, I trust their numbing no matter how trivial it may seem. The advice they give is invisible but not meaningless, although I can barely see to the right of me and up the lobby.

Hallways and stairwells follow my wailing footsteps, sometimes I don't mind this. I run towards them often. The needles prowling my arm are to monitor how imperceptible I've become; Could the world see me if I returned to the cage?

Transitioning back to the enclosure is a ceremony I never gracefully participate in. My body is intangible. Assistants, mostly, walk past my flesh uniform. Some, however, scruff me by my hair and drag me out of the liminal.

Windows Open

The stiff hinges and latches upon my glass portal are difficult to remove. Dehydrated screws create unbalanced expectations that I will be harmed during the procedure. For this reason, I keep the windows closed. Never letting a draft in, never feeling a breeze, never listening to lurid chatters beyond my own.

I gaze from my sorrowful curtain to see a row of panes and glossy panels. Just by marvelling in their direction I invade. I intrude. Their glazed faces become skewed; they shatter. Through apologies, I polish what I can. Sadly, you cannot fix a broken window with polish. Despite that, I clean.

Abrasion creates more cracks, wiping withers the shimmer away. Forever wishing I didn't view through my windows, I plead to barricade myself in darkness. So I may never harm another person with my eyes, never feel their pain as I hurt them, and never listen to lurid screams beyond my own.

Lady Persephone

Persephone, the bloom in the dark,
You waltzed with grace, agitated with a spark.
In the realm of brimstone, a romantic advance,
A crown enclosed in Hades' keep.

A pomegranate's seeds, a tempting plea
An appetite for passion that set her free.
In Hades' arms and Demeter's screams,
A mother rings in her ears,
May she rise amongst silver streams.
Lady, do you wish to vanish like the rest?
Do you taunt yourself with thoughts of
returning?

Sadly, you shine in this world,
A beacon to your whereabouts.
You will be found, forever.
Return back to Hades, Kore
So that you may be respected as an unseen
beauty.

A Layer of Heaven

Swimming in the deep waters,
My soul a raft upon the waves,
Drifting through the murky depths,
In search of a safe haven.
In other quarters of Heaven
A tempest of judgement remains.
But here, in the occultist province,
I wade amongst perceived lunacy,
I begin the craze and continue the panic.
Swim away from the storm,
Seek a paradise untouched.
A layer of Heaven upon my skin,
A layer of Heaven.

Bones / Shaking

Complaining twigs reach for my legs,
Slanted pavements damage my Achilles,
My ankles prepare for crisis and cessation.
Through all the bolts I possess, my feet never
recover,
Snuff out any candle,
collapse all life; my bones shake through earth's
rotation.
A clicking choir screams for assistance,
They make my palpitations muffled,
A true muted symphony.
"Why can't I be like everyone else?"
I shriek.

Why can't I live?
Why can't I breathe?
Why can't I sleep?

Black Dog

Silent and still, the Black Dog sits by the stones of those who left. In the dead of night, his ears go up, watching over those who sleep. He hears the tears they cry, they long to return for another life. No sound does he make, lest he disturb their mourning. But come daybreak, his whimpers can be heard in the dry grass and dried blood.

All who gaze upon his eyes will know that those who lie beneath chose their destination. Their fears won them. Do not think little of those who choose; do not belittle the Black Dog, though the he sits still to us, he will run to and from The Veil for them.

Eden

Eden, the paradise of legend,
She lays muted and stagnant
The flowers once so vibrant,
Now lie dormant and weep
Adam walks amongst dead trees,
His heart heavy like metal,
Eve has been consumed by worlds and has
become a fine dust, like ash, throughout the air
of Eden.

In the still of the broken,
Rustling of the leaves can be heard,
Mourning its own demise.
Under rotten fruit, a Serpent is left to grieve,
Serpent attempts to sooth the spirit by contorting
itself inwards.

Stretching itself thin only forces rivers to dry
out. Without Eve, all must end. And so it will.

As Eden falls into despair,
All that is left is a lingering fear and a prayer.

Leviathan

Hurt and pain are the least of my worries,
Catch my heart and mend my back,
Know me forever, hear my voice crack.

The breaking point of a blank mind is lost to the
abyss,
I remind me of everything I miss.
I remind me that I am not nominal.
I remind you that I cannot return.

"To return would take so much",
No matter how small they made me feel,
No matter how deep this abyss may be,
I look in the ocean's reflection "Just stay with
me."
Just be awake for a little longer...company with
my own divine has never felt so meaningful.

Hurt and pain are the least of my worries,
I am a great beyond that is vast and beautiful.
I am a wise ache that will feel forever, so, may
the waves crash against my eyelashes and let the
moon draw herself closer to me.

I am Leviathan.

Running Races

Please stop running,
My legs are penetrated with an ache. He always
demanded I ran. Always. I ran every playground
day and night as he loved to chase prey. He saw
me as a dog under his command and, for a
while, that was my role.

I was never the Dad or Mum when playing
"House". I was never the children. I was the pet,
the animal, the object. Trying to keep up with
the stories so I felt included. Trying not to scrape
my knees on the cement as I crawled.
Eventually, I stopped crawling, I stood up and
ran.

It's a difficult conflict. Those who know me
would say "He loves to run!". I do. I love to run
alone, for myself and by myself. I've now
developed the fear of being chased, the fear of
falling and catching my skin on the ground, the
fear of my legs disobeying me. Running became
a tactic to keep me from being happy. He made
it so and she made it so. Running became a
method to try and take me away...

So, I stopped running.

My Body; A Vessel

To say i'm disappointed would be an
understatement,
You have baffled me. Twisted me wrong-way
down and outside-in.
Creating wounds on my vessel that no man can
see. Nor witness.
Not once does agonising peace flood the stables
or charge the gates.

To arc my digits, the price I'd pay.
To flourish my hips would make my day,
A generation I must wait to see myself flow like
running water on rapids.
I long for fast pace, they long for "still".
In the same moment, I admit "still" is my wish.
Albeit, "still" is not what I want.

Humans associate "still" with calm; steady. We
say "still" is like being in fields with chaos long
gone. No.
It is not "still" I crave.
How dare you confirm my movement as if it
were your own.
"Still" doesn't make a fraction of my desire.
Freedom.

I fantasise about freedom.

To be the grass in those fields,
To photosynthesise on my own thoughts,
And show those thoughts through movement.
Free of cessation, stale pausing, gasping for air.
Free from the distressing arachnids crawling
endlessly on my seams.
Free dammit.

To say i'm disappointed would be an
understatement,
You have baffled me. Twisted me wrong-way
down and outside-in.
To arc my digits, the price I'd pay.
To flourish my hips would make my day,
A generation I must wait to see myself flow like
running water on rapids.
I am, unfortunately, patient. I am, unfortunately,
hopeful.
I am, unfortunately, strong, and brave, and
smart, and bigger than life.

But not once has agonising peace flood those
stables or charged those gates.

Miss Baphomet

In twisted reverie, I see Baphomet's face,
A reflection of duality's embrace.
As above, so below, in endless grace,
Two worlds entwined, one divine place.

Her horned head, a crown of power and might,
Symbolizes balance, day and night.
Right and left, light and dark, unite,
In perfect harmony, they ignite.

Beneath her gaze, all contradictions fade,
Unity and diversity displayed.
One body, many limbs, diverse and strong,
Together weaving life's cosmic song.

In every aspect, duality shines,
Yin and yang, intertwining lines.
From the microcosm to the macrocosm,
All is connected, forever in bloom.

The Pentagram, a symbol of our quest,
Five elements entwined in unity's nest.
Upward-pointing star, a path to the skies,
Downward-pointing star, roots that arise.

In Miss Baphomet's eyes, the depths of truth,
A mirror to our souls, a voice of youth.
She guides us through life's cycles and spans,
Eternal wisdom, an eternal fan.

So let us embrace this dual nature,
And find balance within life's feature.
For in Baphomet's image we are made,
Reflections of divinity displayed.

A Layer of Hell

Drowning in oceans of darkness, profound,
The realm of eternal suffering and sleep,
Where souls endure endless pain.
And chaos reigns supreme, like a raging bane.

Yet amidst the flames and screams so loud,
I find a strange and eerie calmness proud,
This place, despite its hellish nature, feels like
home to me.
My heart finds solace in the roar of the throne.

The fires that burn bright and fierce within,
Are but a reflection of my own sin,
But here I am not judged or shamed,
For in this pit of despair, I am reclaimed.

So let the demons dance and play their part,
As I embrace the madness of this art,
For in the depths of hell, I find my peace,
A serenity that only here can cease.
A layer of Hell upon my skin,
A layer of Hell.

A Funeral

Amidst the grieving hearts and tear-stained
faces,
I find myself, released from earthly chains,
Eternally resting, devoid of all pains.

At last, the burden of suffering has ceased,
No longer trapped in this mortal lease,
I gaze upon the mourners with tranquil eyes,
Their sorrowful whispers were like distant cries.

I longed for this moment of peace,
To bid farewell to the world's cruel lease,
No more to bear the weight of life's demands,
No more to wander through desolate lands.

In death's embrace, I've found sweet relief,
From the struggles that caused so much grief,
No more to battle the demons within,
No more layers of Heaven to endure.

Please, do not weep for me,
I have found solace, devoid of all fear,
I've journeyed beyond The Veil of the known,
To a realm where souls find solace alone.

I hope, as you mourn and bid me adieu,
That my release from suffering brings comfort to
you,
May my departure inspire a yearning within,
To create a world where pain is rescinded.

May all souls find respite, like mine, painless,
May peace and serenity be their constant
address,
In this grand symphony of life and death,
And as you lay me to rest, let it be known,
In my eternal slumber, I am finally home.

Here Lies

Here lies the final verse, the song of this tome,
A eulogy for endings, bidding farewell to you,
dear reader,
We gather now to honour the inevitable
departure.

With trembling pen and bittersweet refrain,
I offer gratitude for your unwavering embrace,
You, who have traversed the labyrinth of my
thoughts,
Nurturing these verses with your discerning
grace.

Together we've danced amidst metaphorical
skies,
Witnessed the birth of my poetic demise.
Transforming mere ink into a symphony of
emotions,
Breathing life into the melancholy and the sage.

Let it be known that it's you I owe this farewell,
You've welcomed endings with open arms,
You've embraced the transient beauty of a
closing chapter,

And revelled in the echoes of life's fleeting charms.

Here lies the last verse, the final verse we share,
Farewell, my dear reader, until we meet again,
In the pages of another poet's tender embrace,
For it is in the endings that we truly find beginnings,
And it's in the letting go, that we find the utmost grace.